# IRELAND
## in Colour

PHOTOGRAPHS BY KENNETH SCOWEN

INTRODUCTION BY JOHN D. SHERIDAN

B. T. BATSFORD LTD. LONDON

*First published, 1960*

PRINTED IN THE NETHERLANDS
BY L. VAN LEER & CO. LTD., LONDON AND AMSTERDAM
AND BOUND BY DORSTEL PRESS LTD., HARLOW, ESSEX
FOR THE PUBLISHERS

B. T. BATSFORD LTD.
4 FITZHARDINGE STREET, PORTMAN SQUARE, LONDON, W-I

# THE PLATES

# INTRODUCTION

Ireland, Australia, and Argentina are the only countries in the world that have more cattle than human beings. And Ireland's population is not only small but scattered: the only two dark spots on her population map are Dublin and Belfast, which, with roughly a million between them, account for well over a quarter of her entire population. Indeed if weight of human beings could tilt the country over like a boat, Ireland would swing eastward on a north-south axis and the sea would flow in over the flat central plain.

Cork, the next city, has only seventy thousand people, yet Cork is as big as any three of the smaller cities together. The bulk of Ireland's population, then, lives in the rural areas. Ireland has many provincial towns, and many industries – she makes stout, linen, ships, sugar, ropes, cement, leather, and woollens – but agriculture is her principal industry, and apart from her two big cities, and the spatter of linen towns in the north-east, she has no concentrations of industry. The smoke from her factories rises into blue, unclouded air, and once you have left the cities behind there is green country all about you and plenty of elbow room.

Ireland has been described as saucer-shaped, but this description needs to be modified a little, for the mountain rim is not continuous, there are several inland ranges in the south, and on the east coast there is a great lowland stretch reaching from Dublin Bay to the Carlingford Mountains. This opening is the natural outlet for the central plain that stretches west to Galway, north to Cavan, and south to the fertile Golden Vale of

Limerick and Tipperary.

The great plain that is the heart of Ireland is flat and unspectacular but by no means uninteresting. The Boyne valley is a beauty spot in its own right, the north midlands are dotted with lakes, and gorse brightens the great Curragh of Kildare that has been the nursery of so many thorough-breds. The long roads lead through green and pleasant country where towns are few and villages consist mostly of one straggling street. Black bullocks graze behind the hedges, and creamery churns stand on the roadside platforms. But nothing gives a lift to the heart until you cross the Shannon at Athlone; for the central plain is only the curtain-raiser, and the magic does not begin until you reach the threshold of the hills.

In the meantime, however, you will have met the people, and you will have discovered – unless you are very unlucky, or very shy, or very dour – that they are a welcoming, hospitable people. Dr. Johnson said of the Irish that they are a fair-minded people – they never speak well of one another. But they seldom give the hard word to the stranger. For they are very fond of strangers, especially when they are lost, and the surest way of making friends in Ireland is to stop and ask the way. When you do, the first man you speak to will regard you as his own, and whilst he is considering your problem, and giving it his earnest and undivided attention, the neighbours will try to dispute his claim by getting you to re-state your case and forming themselves into *ad hoc* committees. They will weigh up the merits of alternative routes, and advise you for your good; and if things are slack one or two of them may even offer to come a bit of the way with you.

You will be made welcome in Ireland, not just as a tourist who pays us the compliment of not going to France or the Black Forest, but for yourself and as a person. And we don't stand on ceremony, we don't wait for introductions. We will take you to our hearts if you give us half a chance.

There are many things about us that you will discover for yourself. You will discover, for instance, that in Ireland the man is not lost in his office. You will find that the 'boots', the waiters, and the chambermaids are helpful but not obsequious, friendly but not forward, and that they do not look up to you, or down on you, but straight at you. They will give you the respect that hospitality demands, and they will never forget that you are a guest, but they are quite likely to ask you, without taking from your dignity or their own, if you know a good tip for the three-thirty.

Other things about us, you may not discover so easily. You may not notice that we are a self-conscious people. In twos and threes we are fluent and voluble, and in public-house bars we can light a new story from the butt of an old one, but we have to be dragooned into proposing resolutions. In Ireland, everyone goes to the meeting, but it is the devil of a job to get anyone to take the chair.

You will probably think, when you come to Ireland, that life moves at a leisurely pace here, and that the struggle for existence is less strenuous than it is in highly-industrialized countries. But do not be deceived by appearances. We like to have time to stand and stare, and we think it a poor life if a man is too busy to crack a joke or pass the time of day.

We may seem to lack the glib and obvious virtues that are summed up in the word 'business-like', but we have an oblique approach that is just as effective and often more dangerous, and we won't sell our hens on a wet day.

And as a constant overtone to both business and pleasure we like good conversation with a laugh for leavening. You may talk to us about most things and get as good as you give. But please don't talk to us about fairies or leprechauns, as if you were amongst a credulous, superstitious, and child-like people. For we are really a serious people, a hard-headed people. As Chesterton said, we do best at the hard trades – soldiering and the law. We are tolerant as a rule, but in some matters we have a low flashpoint.

So much by way of briefing.

You are out of the midlands now, perhaps, making for the mountains and the western sea. You are in Galway, looking about you before you head north for Connemara and the Corrib country. And you could do worse than stay put for a day or two. For Galway is a gracious city: old, friendly, and picturesque. The Irish-speaking districts of the west are quite close to it, and you may hear snatches of sonorous Gaelic from mountainy men selling calves in Eyre Square. Galway is the capital of the province of Connacht, and the gateway to the west. It sleeps a little now, perhaps, but it has ancient glories to remember, and it still has its Spanish Arch and Spanish Arcade as proof that it was once a great seaport, doing a thriving trade with the Continent, and importing Spanish wine which fetched high prices in London because the longer sea journey was supposed to improve its flavour.

One of the sights of Galway is the gathering of the salmon below the Salmon Weir Bridge on the short Corrib river, waiting their passage inland to more than a thousand square miles of lakes. Another famous gathering takes place in the first days of August, when Galway Race Week brings all Connacht to the city – traders and teachers, farmers and gentry, and ebullient tinkers and gipsies who are described later in the charge sheets as 'persons of the itinerant class'.

Galway was a strong Anglo-Irish colony in its time, and an ancient law ordered that 'neither O nor Mac shall strutte ne swagger in the streets'; but the Os and the Macs must have swaggered once in a while, for there was an inscription on one of the city gates which read: 'From the fury of the O'Flahertys, good Lord deliver us.'

The three Aran Islands – Inishmore, Inishmaan, and Inishere – thirty miles out in Galway Bay, are remote, splendid, and unique. They represent a past that has seeped into and coloured the present, a way of life that has changed little with the centuries; and they exemplify the tenacity and land-hunger of the Gael. In the beginning there was no soil in Aran (the islands are referred to collectively as 'Aran'): there was nothing but the solid rock. The fields of Aran are, quite literally, man-made. Sand and seaweed was carried from the shore, spread on the rocky pavements, and fenced about with high walls of grey stone, lest it should be whisked up by the Atlantic gales and carried out to sea. In time the grass grew, and its roots gave purchase and substance to these pockets, and to-day

Aran is a mosaic of tiny fields, a honeycomb of stone walls.

Aran is itself. There is no other place like it. It has no turf, no rivers, no trees. But its tiny man-made fields raise hardy cattle, the black curraghs of the islanders bring in cod, and lobsters, and herring, and the people live better than many on the mainland. Visitors sometimes ask 'What keeps them here?' It might be better to ask what brings them back, for many of the islanders are 'returned Yankees' who have spent ten years or more in Boston or Hartford and then come back to wear hide shoes and grey homespuns, speak their native Gaelic, and put to sea in fragile, beetle-black curraghs.

Aran is the background to J. M. Synge's tragedy *Riders to the Sea* and to Robert Flaherty's film *Man of Aran*, but it is still as lonely and unspoilt as it was when the first settlers spread carpets of earth on its solid stone. They may well have been monks seeking penance and solitude, for Aran is covered with the ruins of churches, and every acre has its hermit's cell or grey, roofless oratory. There are many prettier places in Ireland, but none so far removed from the world of lights and bustle. When you visit Aran you step back in time and experience a restfulness that is to be found in few places in the world.

North of Galway, and bounded by the Atlantic on one side, and on the other by islanded Lough Corrib, lies the fascinating country of Connemara. This is Connacht at its best, Connacht of the lakes and mountains, of the little stone-walled fields, of the heather, lichens, and mosses, and dominated everywhere by the majestic range of the Twelve Bens. The coast is fretted by the Atlantic, and there is a wealth of fiords, inlets, and headlands. North of Clew Bay, with its bewildering clusters of islands, lies Achill Island, where there are magnificent cliffs and purple mountains. Achill is artists' country. Paul Henry was the first to paint it into fame and to revel in its colours, and he has had hosts of imitators. A feature of Achill is the spectacular white of its cottages, which stand out against the glory of its sunsets and hold the last dregs of light.

Another feature of this lovely island is the hunting of the porbeagle shark, which is a local industry, and which is carried on from a little cove sheltered by Keel Head. And Achill has many such coves, and many such sandy beaches. Here, as all along the Connacht coast, you come across little bays and inlets and feel that you have discovered them; and often you either share them with the seabirds or have them all to yourself. Connacht is an unspoilt province, and every turn of the road brings fresh delights.

But perhaps you have gone south instead of west, and made straight for the Kingdom of Kerry, where the open Atlantic has carved deep inlets and the headlands stand out like finger-posts. Kerry is a wild and beautiful county, richly dowered with noble mountains, but it is not just another Connacht. For here the wildness is tempered a little, the colours have changed subtly, and the softness of the south begins to make itself felt. Ireland's mountain lands are not variations on a basic theme. Each of them has its own special character, each is unmistakeably itself. The charm of Ireland is that it never repeats itself. It is a country of infinite variety, a tiny island but a continent in little.

One of the best introductions to the south-west is the 'Ring of Kerry' tour, a circuit that gives wonderful views of the coast of the Iveragh peninsula, takes in Cahirciveen, Parknasilla, and Kenmare, and brings you your first glimpses of Killarney. Killarney, like Capri, has become a name, and it has been praised so often that many people go there with a stubborn resolve not to be impressed. But in spite of Thomas Moore, who called it 'Heaven's reflex', and said that angels 'fold their wings and rest' there, in spite too of the many lesser lyricists who have made it rhyme with 'blarney', Killarney does not disappoint.

The journey from Killarney to Glengarriff is one which no one should miss. You go to Kenmare by way of Lady's View, and then you cross the Caha Mountains by the twisting Healy Pass with its high Calvary. All this is wild and lovely scenery, and you could linger with profit at a dozen spots on the way. Glengarriff itself, which is built on an inlet of Bantry Bay, is regarded as one of the glories of the south. And here you notice another change in the scenery. Munster is not Connacht, but Munster is not all of a piece. It has shades and gradations. It varies from valley to valley, almost from parish to parish.

Glengarriff takes you by surprise. You reach it by a wild and rocky road, but you find luxuriant vegetation, an unexpected warmth, and a blue, Mediterranean sea. Glengarriff has a profusion of sub-tropical trees and shrubs that are really indigenous to the place but seem to be collectors' items imported to make a botanical garden on the shores of Bantry Bay.

The river-valleys of the Bandon, Lee, and Blackwater offer a striking contrast to the mountainous coastal regions of Cork and Kerry. Here is some of the richest land in Ireland: creamery country, beef country, wheatlands and clover fields. The Blackwater Valley is particularly beautiful, and many a great house looks down on its famous salmon-stretches. It was here that the settlers picked their big estates and lived graciously on planted acres. One of the Elizabethan settlers was Sir Walter Raleigh, who lived at Myrtle Grove, in Youghal. His house is still standing, and it was in its gardens that he puffed the first pipe ever smoked in Ireland and planted the first potatoes.

In jumping from Youghal to Dublin I make no apology. The wonder is that I held off so long. For anyone writing about Ireland has to fight against the temptation of bringing in Dublin too soon, just as every visitor to Ireland has to fight against the temptation of staying in Dublin too long. Dublin is a city with everything to recommend it – wide streets, stately Georgian houses, suburbs that stretch along the bay, and beaches and bathing places all the way from Howth to Dun Laoghaire. (I know a Dublin man who manages to have a bathe during his hour-and-a-half mid-day break, and have dinner at home after it.)

But none of these assets can explain the charm of Dublin. We must throw in Moore Street, with it raucous, quick-witted hawkers; Croke Park, where on All-Ireland Final days deep-chested hurlers from Tipperary and Kilkenny thrill the crowds, and Kerry footballers rise like swallows when they are fielding a high ball; the curving road near the Magazine Fort in the Phoenix Park, from which, on summer evenings, one looks down on the swans and the racing eights on the Liffey; the plays of Sean O'Casey and the gong that signals the rise of the curtain at the Abbey. And we must not forget the ghosts of the past: Mangan and Moore; Flood and Grattan; Swift and Shaw; Goldsmith and Richard Brinsley Sheridan; Handel and Rowan Hamilton. Some of the Georgian houses are tenements now (though there are fewer tenements in Dublin than in many big cities), but many of them have changed but little from the days when there were sedan chairs in Merrion Square.

Dublin has all the advantages of a big city, and the friendliness of a small town. It has no pall of smoke, no choking fogs, no coat of grime. Its churches and public buildings are set to catch the eye, but its factories are discreetly hidden. It is not an industrial city, and it lives on its hinterland – which is the whole scatter of the central plain. It has good pubs, good theatres, good hotels, and good conversation, and although it is a thriving modern city it gives the impression of leisure and gracious living and wears a holiday air.

The truth must be told: Dublin is a holiday city, and Belfast is not. Belfast is to Dublin, except in point of size, as Glasgow is to Edinburgh. Belfast works for its living, and is not ashamed of it; Dublin plays at being a gentleman with private means. Belfast does not hide its tall factories, and it cannot hide its gantries. It answers the scream of the siren and makes its money from clanging hammers and rattling looms. It has a background of green hills, and its suburbs spread out along the banks of the lough. It has a vigorous cultural life, and it is not without fine buildings. It is the gateway to Antrim, and there is beauty in plenty along the Down coast from Bangor to Rostrevor.

16

Compared with Dublin, Belfast is of recent growth – during the nine-teenth century, for instance, its population, which was only 500 in the year 1600, grew from 25,000 to 300,000. But if Dublin boasts of its age, Belfast can point to Bangor; for though Dublin is old, Bangor is older still. Bangor is a flourishing seaside resort, thirteen miles from Belfast, but it is also the site of St. Comgall's sixth-century monastery which in its day was famous throughout all Europe and attracted students from Britain, Gaul, and the Rhineland.

And later, when the barbarian inroads had almost quenched religion and learning on the Continent, it was monks from Bangor and places like it – from Clonmacnoise, and Clonard, and Durrow, and Derry – who re-lit the almost extinguished flame and built monasteries in Gaul and Switzerland and Lombardy. Nor was Britain overlooked, and it was an English historian, not an Irish, who said that it was Aidan and not Augus-tine who was the real apostle of England; and the Venerable Bede, who seldom had anything good to say of the Celts, acknowledged that 'the children of the English received from Aidan's monks an education as complete as that which was to be had in any of the great Irish monas-teries.'

All this may seem very far removed from Belfast, with its shipyards and foundries, but in Ireland the past is part of the present. The Irish are often accused of having long memories, but we have good reason to remember that Ireland was once 'the Island of Saints and Scholars', for in Ireland the ruins of the Christian past are everywhere, and the names of the great monasteries, and of the saints who taught in them, are familiar to the men stooking hay in the fields.

I may be a little biased in favour of Dublin at the expense of Belfast, and you must add and subtract marks accordingly. But I have tried to be fair. For I have a liking for this northern city. It speaks its mind and does not pretend. It pays its way. It straddles a noble lough and it is the gateway to the highlands of the north-east and the glorious Antrim coast. All this is wonderful country, with magnificent scenery all the way to Portrush and Portstewart.

I hope that I have atoned for my sin (I have at least acknowledged it) and made some amends to Belfast, but there is worse to come. When I cross the narrow neck of land that separates Lough Foyle from Lough Swilly I am in country about which I am really bigoted; for Donegal is the county that I know best and love best, and although I say it myself it is not the least among the counties of Ireland.

The great gash of the Swilly, that majestic sea-going lough that is swept by the Atlantic tides, borders a wonderland that stretches right round to Donegal Bay on the west coast: Mulroy Bay and Sheephaven; Carrigart, Downings, and Rosapenna; Bunbeg and Bloody Foreland; the sudden peak of flinty Errigal and the long hog-back of Muckish. If you want mountain and sea, lake and glen, and a hundred changing colours of earth and sky, you will find them here as surely and as plentifully as in Kerry or Connemara. And this is not the west or the south. This is Donegal, and it might be a new country. Ireland has a thousand faces.

In Donegal, too, you will find a different people; cousins to those you have met already, perhaps, but with distinctive characteristics; a warm-hearted, clannish people, not as quick to make friends as the Munster folk are, but eternally and fanatically loyal to those they do make.

I could go on like this for a long time, but it might be better to stop before I commit myself too deeply; for I know that my bias is showing.

Besides, there is much that I have no space to mention, and whole counties must go by default. I have said nothing about Kilkee, and the Cliffs of Moher, and Lisdoonvarna, in County Clare; about Waterford's Tramore or Wicklow's Glendalough and Avoca; about the Erne Lakes of Fermanagh and the orchards of Armagh and Kilkenny. I have left Dublin without bringing you to see the pageantry of the Horse Show, or the glorious sweep of Killiney Bay; I have ignored the Cork Film Festival and the annual week of grand opera in the ancient city of Wexford.

Perhaps it is just as well. In an introduction such as this, as in the set of pictures that follows it, the choice of subjects must be arbitrary to some extent. If we tried to show more, we might end up by showing less; for Ireland is more than the sum of its parts, and it cannot be reduced to a formula or tabulated like an inventory. Beyond and above all the pictures there is the composite picture that cannot be set down in words or colours.

The pictures, no doubt, will speak for themselves, and say different things to different people, but there is a case for a commentary. The chairman's speech must not obtrude, but it serves a purpose. For Ireland is a country that has not so much been presented to the world as misrepresented – not in malice but with well-intentioned sentimentality –

and the picture that emerges from travellers' tales, novels, and plays, is one that never was on land or sea. A world that has grown too old for fairies and leprechauns wants to believe in them by proxy; a world bedevilled by mergers and preference shares likes to feel that in one un-progressive island the hens are still free to walk about the kitchen and the pig has the run of the parlour.

People who have been reared on these notions of Ireland would be well advised – if they want to retain their illusions – to stay at home and re-read *Handy Andy*, or go to New York and watch the St. Patrick's Day Parade; for if they come to Ireland thinking in terms of bogs and blarney, red petticoats and twirling shillelaghs, 'bulls' and four-leafed shamrock and Donnybrook Fair, they will certainly be disappointed. Romantic Ireland, in this sense, is dead and gone; it's with Lover in the grave. Ireland, for good or ill, has moved with the times. The colleens wear nylons; the young men – some of them at least – wear duffel coats and crew cuts; and electricity pylons are threaded round the shoulders of the hills.

You can have as much quietness as you want in Ireland, but you are not condemned to quietness. You can spend your days on lonely beaches or by wild mountain lakes, but when the sun goes down you are always within easy reach of cinemas and dance bands. And there is no shortage of creature comforts: good shops, good hotels, and good food. You can also have good drink, if the humour takes you. Irish bars and lounges are pleasant places. They will serve you with the local brew, if you want it, but no one will look surprised if you prefer the drinks that you see advertised on French hoardings. You may even ask for Scotch whisky – and get it – for we are a tolerant people and we like to flatter our visitors. We drink Irish whiskey ourselves, but we live and let live, and we will admit if we are put to it that Scotch is the best of the temperance drinks.

Ireland has been called 'the green isle', and the label is more than a poetic fancy: her limestone soil and her adequate rainfall (the euphemism is as soft and kindly as Irish rain) have given her grass of a vivid green that is peculiar to herself. This intensity of colour, too, extends to her skies and lakes, to heather and bogland, fiord and mountain slope. Ireland is a land of colours. The granite outcrops of the coast are brightened by blood-red fuchsia bushes, and the golden furze is everywhere. Film directors sometimes grumble about our Irish weather, but they give thanks for the colours it brings to the countryside. (We tell a story about one of them, who, as his plane circled before landing at Shannon, said 'My, what a green country!' Then he added: 'But what are those black spots I see here and there?' 'If they move', said an Irishman who was sitting near him, 'they're crows. It they don't, they're county council workers.')

Other countries have green belts—to curb their builders and give lungs to their cities – but Ireland's green belt stretches from shore to shore, and the absence of any concentration of heavy industries has left her coastline unsullied. The straight roads of the central plain run unhindered to the sea and give easy access to the glories of the south-western and western coasts from Kinsale to Bloody Foreland; the open Atlantic washes the northern shore from Tory Island to Rathlin; whilst along the east coast, and right round to Cork City, there is no smoke to speak of save at Belfast and Dublin.

But Ireland is history as well as geography. She is the last outpost of western Europe, and she was the only part of it that did not hear the tramp of the Roman legions. But she never held herself aloof from Europe, and she shared its cultural inheritance. Her missionary monks are still remembered from the Loire to the heel of Italy, and in later centuries her scholars and priests were trained in Rome, Louvain, and Salamanca. She built up a distinctive civilization, but it was not an alien civilization. The colouring was Celtic, but the design was part of the broad European pattern.

But to say that the Irish are a Celtic people is even more of a generalization than to say that the English are Anglo-Saxons. The truth is that we are a mixture. We banished the Danes — with considerable difficulty — after they had been with us for two centuries, but remnants of them stayed behind as traders and became fused with the Irish nation. So too, the Normans in their time became 'more Irish than the Irish themselves'. The invaders conquered by force of arms, but they were themselves conquered by something stronger than arms, and Viceroy after Viceroy attempted in vain to wean the great Anglo-Irish barons from the native customs, dress, and language.

The Normans learned Irish, and we learned English — long centuries later. But in adopting it we changed it. We made it our own, as surely as we made the Danes and the Normans our own. We moulded it to suit the Irish mind. We invigorated it with the Irish idiom. We visited on it a great sea-change. We gave it new sounds, new overtones of meaning. We married it with poetry and made it rich, decorative, musical. In short, we made it our own.

The chairman has been on his feet long enough, and it is time that he sat down; for this is primarily a book of pictures, not a book of words. We are almost finished with special pleading. The camera must take over now, and the camera does not try to shape your verdict or bespeak your good will. It deals with facts. It records what it sees, faithfully and objectively, and leaves you to judge for yourself.

But even the best of pictures have their limitations. They tell a graphic story, but they cannot tell the whole story. They capture colours that cannot be translated satisfactorily into black words on white paper, and they give you images of reality instead of muffled symbols. They show you lake and mountain, gorse and heather, and give you fascinating glimpses of a lovely country. But they leave something unsaid, for the best they can do is to show you Ireland as mass and bulk, light and shade; and though this is a very good best indeed, it cries out for the complement of human speech. I am very glad to sit down now and let Ireland speak for herself, but I make no apology for having introduced her at some length; for Ireland is not just a geographical entity, a pattern of high land and low land, bog and meadow, but a people and a way of life.

*Evening at Killarney*

The three lakes which are the heart of Killarney are sur-
rounded by wooded slopes of oak, cedar, and holly, and a profusion
of ferns and shrubs; and all about is a vast backdrop of mountains.
The lakes look well in rain or sunshine, mist or shadow, but perhaps
they look best on the verge of the gloaming, when the colours of
water, sky, and mountain change from moment to moment.
Most of the Lake District is now included in the National Park,
formerly the 10,000-acre Muckross Estate, and the best composite
view of the whole region is that from Aghadoe, near the northern
shore of the Lower Lake – 'where the apple falls in the salmon's eye'.
When presenting Killarney to the Irish nation, the former owner of
Muckross said: 'I hope it becomes the greatest playground in the
world – for there is not another like it, and I know them all.'

## Macgillycuddy's Reeks, Co. Kerry

The Reeks are separated from the Killarney mountains proper (Tomies and the Purple Mountain group) by the wild Gap of Dunloe, a magnificent defile that runs for seven miles between the two ranges. From the Gap there are splendid views of the Reeks, and the bugles of the guides wake long-fading echoes from the hills. (Tennyson was remembering Killarney when he wrote 'Blow, bugle, blow, set the wild echoes flying.')

The traditional tour of Killarney takes a full day, and is done in stages: by sidecar to 'Kate Kearney's Cottage'; by pony (the only form of transport permitted) through the Gap; and by boat through the three lakes.

26

## Glenbeigh, Co. Kerry

The road from Cahirciveen to Glenbeigh, on the famous
'Ring of Kerry', is one of the loveliest stretches in the south-west.
Glenbeigh itself – the name means the Glen of the Birches – fringes
Dingle Bay, and is separated from Caragh Lake (which lies west of
the Macgillycuddy range) by Seefin, a mountain that has associations
with Fionn, the great hero of the old Celtic wonder-tales.
In this colourful region there is some of the finest mountain scenery
in the Kingdom of Kerry, and a fascinating ridge walk on the Macgillycuddy peaks – Carrantuohill (3414 feet), Beenkeragh, Skregmore,
and Caher. And there is good trout fishing everywhere, notably in
Caragh Lake and in the Behy and Caragh rivers.

*Rossbeigh*

Two miles from Glenbeigh, the narrow peninsula of Rossbeigh (the headland of the Birches) stretches north into Dingle Bay, matching – and almost meeting – the peninsula of Inch on the opposite side of the inlet.

Rossbeigh offers miles of sandy beach, excellent bathing, and as much solitude as anyone could wish for.

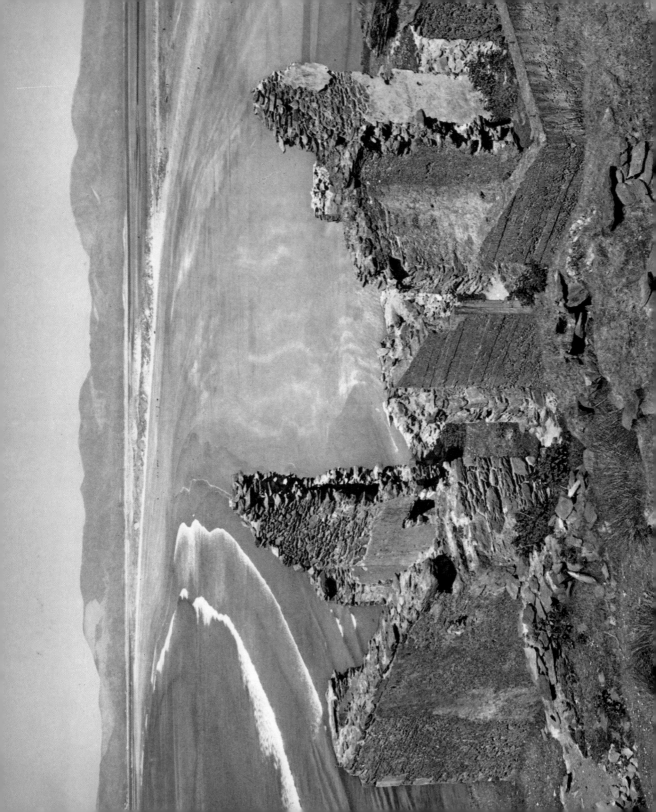

*Cottage near Parknasilla*

Irish houses have grown bigger and better in the last twenty-five years, but you still come across whitewashed cottages like this in the mountain country – and Parknasilla is certainly in the mountain country, for it is one of the stages on the Ring of Kerry, a hundred-mile circuit of the broad Iveragh peninsula. When you 'do the Ring' you start – and finish – at Kenmare or Killarney as you please. Either way you travel an enchanted road.

Parknasilla is a sunny, sheltered cove on the shores of the lovely Kenmare River inlet. It grows exotic shrubs that suggest the Mediterranean rather than the Atlantic, and it might well be a corner of the Riviera.

## Glengarriff, Co. Cork

Glengarriff, which is thirty-six miles from Killarney – by way of the Kenmare River and the corkscrew Healy Pass – is hemmed in between the mountains and the great gash of Bantry Bay.

The name means the wild or rugged glen, but though Glengarriff is rocky and remote, its aspect is benign rather than barren; for it borders a blue, islanded sea, and it is noted for its mild climate, and for its palms, fuchsias, rhododendrons, and sub-tropical shrubs. One of its many beauty spots is the Poulgorm, or Blue Pool, and there are exquisite ornamental gardens on Garnish Island, at the entrance to the harbour.

In recent years, Glengarriff has become popular with American cruising liners, but it is still as secluded and unspoilt as when Bernard Shaw came there to finish *Saint Joan*.

## Cork on the Lee

Cork, the natural outlet for the rich river valleys of Munster, is a pleasant, friendly city, inhabited by a proud, quick-witted, and hospitable people. For the visitor, it is a convenient centre for the show places of the south – the valleys of the Lee and Blackwater, Glengarriff and the Kingdom of Kerry.

The spires we see here are not those of Shandon Church – whose chimes have found their way into so many anthologies – but of St. Finbarr's Cathedral. Finbarr, the patron of Cork, founded a school and monastery in the sixth century on the site of Cork's University College, which has taken for its motto: 'Where Finbarr taught, let Munster learn.'

## Blarney Castle, Co. Cork

From the top of Blarney Castle, a good hundred feet up, there is a fine view of wooded Muskerry; and it was a McCarthy, a chief of this district, who fobbed off the Lord Deputy so often with 'fair words and soft speech' that the exasperated Queen Elizabeth, tired of a post-dated submission that had no sincerity to meet it, is said to have described McCarthy's blandishments as 'blarney' and so given a new word to the language.

Blarney is only five miles from Cork city, and is in the heart of a lovely countryside. It attracts streams of visitors, who come to kiss the stone embedded in the battlements of its fifteenth-century castle, but acquire none of McCarthy's fluency, and go away convinced that the legend is all my eye and Betty Martin.

## A Farmstead near Blarney

This farm might be anywhere in Ireland – a country whose wealth lies in good limestone soil and the green grass that grows from it.

A 'strong farm' like this one might produce bullocks for export and beet for the Mallow sugar factory. And like so many other Irish farms, it will have moved with the times. For the tractor is ousting the plough-horse, and in many a barn the trap that used to bring the family to church on Sundays is lying mildewed, with its shafts pointing forlornly to the roof; whilst the son of the man who used to drive it has a gadget in his pocket for measuring the gaps of his sparking plugs.

*Thomond Bridge and St. John's Castle, Limerick*

At Limerick, the Shannon becomes tidal, but it still has some miles to go before it broadens into its sixty-mile estuary; and it has already come a long way, widened into three lakes, and turned the electricity turbines at Ardnacrusha, eighteen miles from the city.
The castle at Thomond Bridge was built by order of King John, who visited Limerick in 1210. Little of the original structure still stands, and the walls show signs of the pounding they took from Ginkle's artillery during the Williamite Wars.
Limerick is the nearest centre of population to Shannon Airport at Rineanna, which is still, as it was when it was first christened, 'the Plain of the Birds', though the noise of engines has frightened the wild duck and made the honking geese seek quieter havens.

## The Rock of Cashel

This great limestone rock stands high above the rich plain of Tipperary and is one of the most prominent landmarks of the Golden Vale. Cashel has always played a part in the history of Munster. It was the seat of the kings of the province from the fourth century, and it was presented to the Church in the twelfth.

The gem of Cashel is the incomparable Cormac's Chapel, which is the most perfect example of the Irish Romanesque style. There is also a tenth-century round tower and a thirteenth-century cathedral.

In 1496, the cathedral was burned by one of the turbulent Earls of Kildare, and he later excused himself to Henry VII by saying that he had thought the Archbishop was inside.

44

## *Looking Down at Dublin*

Dublin has the sea at its feet and the hills at its elbow. At Rathfarnham, five miles from the city centre, the foothills begin, and from the slopes of the Dublin Mountains you can look down on the roofs of the city and the curve of the bay. Higher up, the 'Featherbed Pass' leads to Glencree, Glendalough, and the 'garden county' of Wicklow.

On the brow of Mount Pelier, the nearest hill to the city, stand the ruins of the 'Hell Fire Club', where the roistering eighteenth-century bloods are said to have foregathered; and just outside Rathfarnham the poet Yeats lived towards the end of his life – 'in an old house, with lovely grounds, and a bridge which spans a stream fresh from the golden granite of the hills.'

46

## The Dublin Custom House

From O'Connell Bridge, the view of the Custom House, Dublin's finest public building, is obstructed by the girders of an overhead railway bridge. Seen from the south quays, at the limit of the steamer berthage, it shows to better advantage.

This superb building, which was completed in 1791 to the design of James Gandon, was almost completely destroyed in the fighting of 1921. Later, however, it was very faithfully restored in the spirit of the original.

The figure of Hope stands on the dome, which is a prominent landmark. Beneath it, on the quays and on the river, are accessories of an industry that was started long before Gandon drew his plans – a Guinness barge, a Guinness boat, and metal containers ready for shipment.

*The Four Courts, Dublin*

The Four Courts, which stands on the northern quays, about a mile west of O'Connell Bridge, and half-way between the city centre and the Phoenix Park, is another of Gandon's masterpieces – he revised and altered the plans after the first architect died; and, like the more famous Custom House, it was badly damaged during 'the Trouble' and excellently restored.

The Liffey is quiet here and carries little traffic, save for the swans that move serenely down-stream from Islandbridge, and a Guinness barge once in a while. Looking at the Four Courts from the bridge beside it one gets the feeling of a city which still retains much of the gracious air of Georgian times.

## Monasterboice, Co, Louth

The Boyne Valley, thirty miles north of Dublin, is a sylvan countryside rich in memories. Amongst its many places of historic interest are Tara, the city and palace of the kings; the Bronze Age burial-place of Bru na Boinne; and Monasterboice, with its round tower and early stone crosses.

Muireadach's Cross, the east face of which is seen here, dates from the tenth century. It is the finest example of the Irish scriptural cross, and is remarkable for the intricacy of its carvings.

The central motif is the Last Judgment, with the good on the right side of the figure and the damned on the left. Notice the devil on the left kicking a soul into hell! Immediately underneath, Michael the Archangel is testing souls in the balance; and a devil lying on his back is tipping up one side of the scale. The bottom panel shows Adam and Eve, and Cain and Abel.

The cross is 17 feet 8 inches high, and a panel on the west face bears the inscription *Or do Muireadach las ndearnad in Chros* – 'A prayer for Muireadach, who caused the cross to be made.'

*The Mountains of Mourne, Co. Down*

The granite ridge of the Mournes dominates the peninsula that lies between Dundrum Bay and Carlingford Lough. Between the hills and the sea, the little towns lie snugly: Warrenpoint and Rostrevor on Carlingford Lough, and within easy reach of Newry; the fishing villages of Kilkeel and Annalong, on the open sea; and Newcastle, a thriving holiday resort with a championship golf course, lying in the shadow of Slieve Donard, the highest mountain in Ulster. All this is lovely country, marking a transition stage between the flat coasts of the central plain and the mountain lands of Ulster.

## Annalong, Co. Down

Annalong, the 'Ford of the Ships', is a picturesque fishing village on the coast road that runs south from Newcastle and curves into Newry along the northern shore of Carlingford Lough. The words 'picturesque' and 'fishing village' seem to run together inevitably, for when you visit a little harbour like this, whether it is in Brittany, or on the Basque coast of Spain, or in the shadow of the Mournes, you wish that you had some skill with the brushes or colour film in your camera.

Annalong is a quiet place, where men mend nets and sit on upturned baskets; but it has its share of excitement, for it is the headquarters of the herring fleet and it wakens into life when the little ships come home.

56

## The City Hall, Belfast

This handsome Renaissance-style building occupies a central position in a city that grew up with the Industrial Revolution, a city of ships and linen, tobacco and cordage, tall factories and lunch-time whistles.

But though it is work-a-day it is not grim or forbidding. Historic Cave Hill looks down on it kindly, and there is green country all about it. The Ards peninsula, which turns out and down like a hanging arm, is dotted with pleasant seaside towns; and to the north is the famous Antrim coast road, which runs close to the water's edge for most of the way to Cushendall and Portrush, with a succession of cliffs and bays and headlands.

## Portmuck, Islandmagee, Co. Antrim

The narrow, seven-mile-long peninsula of Islandmagee forms the seaward shore of Larne Lough. It can be reached inland from Whitehead, at the northern tip of Belfast Lough, or by ferry from Larne.

Its principal attraction is its fine caves and basalt cliffs. At the foot of the Gobbins, the most interesting stretch of the cliffs, there is a fascinating pathway which leads to caves and tunnels and is carried over chasms by tiny bridges.

Near the Gobbins, and almost at the tip of the peninsula, is the little seaside village of Portmuck.

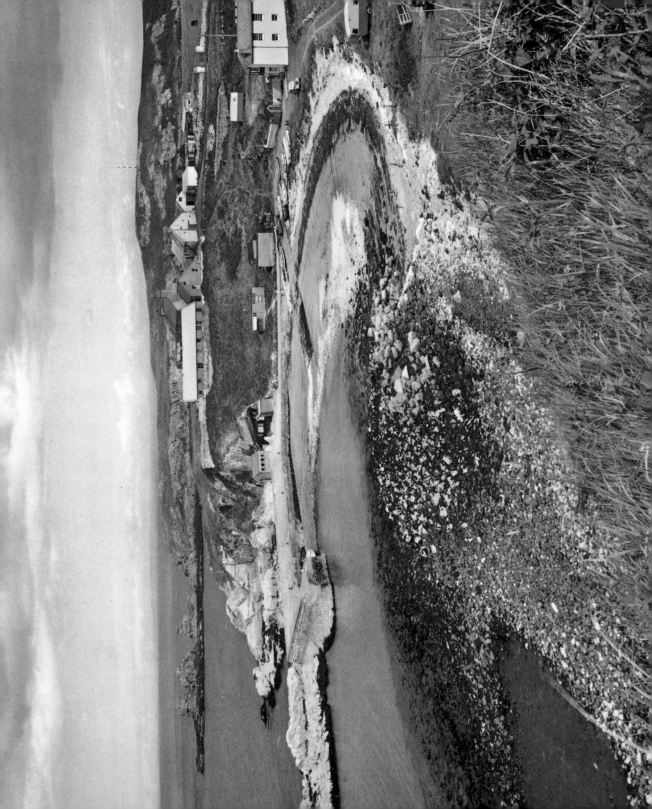

## Glenariff, Co. Antrim

'The Glens' (there are nine of them in all) are Antrim's boast, and the loveliest of them is Glenariff, which runs for five miles inland, and meets the sea at Red Bay, with its chalk and sandstone cliffs, between Cushendall and Garron Point. The road runs half-way up the slope, and from it one looks down on green cultivated bottom lands and up at the flat table-top of the mountain.

There is good trout-fishing in the Glenariff River, which has many fine waterfalls. The most picturesque fall in Glenariff, however, the 'Tears of the Mountain', comes tumbling down to the river from the height above.

At the seaward end of the glen is the village of Waterfoot, near which the Antrim coast road passes through the 'Red Arch' tunnel in the sandstone cliffs.

## The Giant's Causeway, Co. Antrim

The Giant's Causeway, which lies eight miles from the progressive seaside resort of Portrush, and three from the distillery-town of Bushmills, is one of the world's geological wonders. Mythology brings giants into the story, but the real architect was a volcanic eruption of the earth's crust, a mighty disturbance covering an area stretching from the Irish coast to the Scottish island of Skye. The cooling of the lava produced these remarkable rock formations, mainly hexagonal and pentagonal, with their incredible organ-pipe regularity.

## *Sheephaven Bay and Muckish Mountain, Co. Donegal*

Round Sheephaven and its adjoining inlet, Mulroy Bay, is one of the most delightful districts in Donegal—perhaps in all Ireland—and a cluster of lovely resorts: Carrigart, Downings, Port-na-Blagh, and Dunfanaghy.

Carrigart is built on the neck of the Rosguill peninsula, close to the famous Rosapenna golf links; and a little further on, Downings, which is famous for its sands and its sunsets, looks out on Sheephaven and the distant ridge of Muckish.

The 'Atlantic Drive' round the wild Rosguill peninsula fringes Trana-rossan Bay, with its exhilarating ocean breakers, and is a succession of breath-taking views of the open Atlantic and islanded Mulroy.

66

*Lough Inagh, Co. Galway*

Connemara, the part of Galway that lies between Lough Corrib and the Atlantic, is a land of lakes and mountains and wide vistas, dominated everywhere by the majestic range of the Twelve Bens.

Lough Inagh, in the very heart of Connemara, stretches along a deep, glaciated valley between the Bens and the Maamturk Mountains, with Leenane, Kylemore, and Letterfrack within easy distance. But these are only names chosen at random from a long litany, and they do not by any means constitute a hierarchy. You cannot go wrong in Connemara or the wild and lovely country about it, and you will find beauty everywhere between Lough Corrib and the sea.

*Peat Bog near Maam Cross, Co. Galway*

Maam Cross, on the road from Oughterard – a convenient centre for the Corrib fishing – to Recess and Clifden, marks the junction where the road branches off through the wild 'Joyce's Country'. In recent years, Ireland's bigger bogs have been developed commercially, and machine-won turf is providing power for factories and electricity stations; but the smaller bogs are still as God made them, lovely with white *ceannabhan* and purple heather. In the flat midlands the bogs as a rule are dull and featureless, but in the mountainy districts of the west they have a magic of their own.